WALKING DOWN THE ALLEY

HARSHITA VERMA

Copyright © Harshita Verma
All Rights Reserved.

This book has been published with all efforts taken to make the material error-free after the consent of the author. However, the author and the publisher do not assume and hereby disclaim any liability to any party for any loss, damage, or disruption caused by errors or omissions, whether such errors or omissions result from negligence, accident, or any other cause.

While every effort has been made to avoid any mistake or omission, this publication is being sold on the condition and understanding that neither the author nor the publishers or printers would be liable in any manner to any person by reason of any mistake or omission in this publication or for any action taken or omitted to be taken or advice rendered or accepted on the basis of this work. For any defect in printing or binding the publishers will be liable only to replace the defective copy by another copy of this work then available.

This book is dedicated to my 16 year old self, the lovely readers especially my teenage audience.

Contents

Foreword

This is my story, the story of a teenager going through very common stuff so it could just as easily be your story too. We're all in this together; trust me on that.

I've never done anything like writing a book before so I'm just going to jump in.

Preface

The incident recorded in this book really occured in my life as a teenage. Chapter 1; As a 16 year old, this was a petrified task to go through. Although my book is intented mainly for the acknowledgement of boys and girls i hope it will not be shunned by men and women on that account, for part of my plan is to pleasantly remind the readers about the day-to-day disgusting things happening around any other kid and of how one feels about it.

    THE AUTHOR

Acknowledgements

Two people made this book eminently more readable that it otherwise might have been- Paulo coelho & Arpita verma.

Paulo coelho is my inspiration and the reason i started writing in the first place. His books like *The Alchemist, Brida & Like the flowing river* have motivated me to do something remarkable and far from ordinary.

I would like to acknowledge my gratitude to Arpita verma, my sister who is 5 years older than me. I would not be able to get my work done without the continual support of her. When everyone else used to laugh at my poems she was the one who stood for me. She made me a better version of myself and has been incredibly helpful with the detailed editing and adopted the book as her own to put extraordinary efforts in it. Thankyou and i love you.

Walking down the Alley

"*She was walking down the way*
living a pretty solitary life
chased by a creepy hombre
wearing a disguise
He was inquiring about a roadway
although she didn't like
showed him the pathway
with a feeling of despise
She was gradually walking away
in a sentiment of fright
stalked the nerdy guy
grisly and slight
She was turning around the alley
saw him within the sight
fondling his own genitals
in a broad daylight
Created the suspicion of sensual assault
hence rushed in affright
mother questioned her dismay
but she remained quiet."

She dreamt of

She dreamt of satisfaction
and a luxurious life,
She couldn't figure out her fascination
so she wanted a second life.

A woman's beauty

*"A woman's beauty is in her grace
not just in her face
Her soul is a garden of blaze
that he used to embrace
Her charm is in her heart
her beauty is an art."*

Remember...

Woman, you are fearless and sweet
agonizing blood you bleed
You were born with wisdom to heal
before none should you kneel
Woman, adorn yourself with a crown
in a bright green gown
Remember you are the queen
beautiful and serene.

End Matter

Dear fellow reader,

I'm glad you have read all my four poems. You must have understood the message brought to you by these poems which is to be confident about yourself and *be you*.

"Call yourself a queen as it's your name and don't forget to take your claim"

Thankyou so much for sparing some time to read this book.